NEXUS

Information Network

Epris E. Ezekiel

Copyright 2024© Epris E. Ezekiel

All rights reserved. This book is copyrighted and no part of it may be reproduced, distributed, or transmitted in any form or by any means, including photocopying, recording, or other electronic or mechanical methods, without the prior written permission of the publisher, except in the case of brief quotations embodied in critical reviews and certain other non-commercial uses permitted by copyright law.

Printed in the United States of America Copyright 2024© Epris E. Ezekiel

Contents

Chapter 1 1
History 1
Chapter 2 5
What is a Computer Network? 5
Chapter 3 12
Key Objectives of Building and Deploying a Computer Network
.... 12
Chapter 4 20
Best Practices in Computer Network Management 20
Chapter 5 28
Network Management Systems' Features and Deployment .. 28
Chapter 6 31
Common types of networking attacks 31
Chapter 7 35
The Fundamentals of Network Security 35
Chapter 8 43
Challenges of Modern Network Management 43
Conclusion 45

Chapter 1

History

Computer networks are among the greatest technological inventions in human history, and they have had a tremendous impact on people's lives. Before the development of the network, if you wanted to treat yourself to a cloth, you had to go down to the store. Today, however, a simple click on a purchasing website will suffice to obtain your desired item. If you're new to networking, studying its history will help you understand how we got here, step by step.

The network has an interesting history. To comprehend the importance of the network, it is crucial to learn about its origin.

In the 1950s, computers were prohibitively expensive, and not everyone could afford one. However, many processing systems allow multiple users to access computational resources at the same time. The Time-Sharing System was first proposed in the mid to late

1950s. In the Time-Sharing System, each computer user is assigned a terminal that includes a monitor and a keyboard. These terminals are connected to the computer via the controlling route. However, it was still not a full computer network. This system does not support computer-to-computer connections.

Computer networks can trace their origins back to the 1960s when the telephone network served as the primary network. The telephone network mostly uses circuit switching to transmit data from the sender to the receiver. During the height of the Cold War, the United States sought a comprehensive communication network. As a result, a new network model was proposed: a packet-switching network.

Paul Baran introduced the concept of "Message Blocks," while Donald Davies presented "Packet Switching." Packet switching is a method for dividing data into packets that will be transferred over a network. Every time the device sends data to another, it divides it into smaller chunks and chooses the most effective route. If one route fails, it will select another route to continue transmitting packets. Packet switching ensures that data transmission is not interrupted due to a network failure.

Larry Roberts devised the first patch-switching network, ARPAnet, which serves as the foundation for today's Internet. These patch switches were referred to as Interface Message Processors. Every ARPAnet-connected computer must be connected to an IMP device.

ALOHAnet, Telenet, and Tymnet were among the many packet-switching networks established in the mid-1970s. APRAnet was a closed network. Every ARPAnet-connected computer must be connected to an IMP device. The major challenge with ARPAnet is communication between IMP and other sorts of hosts, hence the "1822 Protocol" was developed. However, this protocol cannot provide simultaneous communication between many applications. To address this issue, the NCP protocol was designed. The more versatile TCP/IP protocol superseded NCP in 1983, ushering in the modern Internet.

In 1973, Robert Metcalfe created the Ethernet idea, which subsequently evolved into Local Area Networks (LANs).

In the 1990s, the Internet continued to grow and improve. APRAnet never existed, and NSFNET became the primary network that connected the US network to the international network. Furthermore, in 1990, The World became the world's first commercial Internet Service Provider (ISP), and the commercial ISP business expanded rapidly. In 1991, Merit, IBM, and MCI formed a non-profit corporation to take over NSFNET and rename it ANSNet.

The introduction of the World Wide Web was another significant development in the 1990s. The World Wide Web helps millions of individuals throughout the world have access to the Internet, whether at home or work. The Web also encourages the creation of new applications such as streamed multimedia and other information services.

Chapter 2

What is a Computer Network?

A computer network is a system that allows two or more computing devices to communicate and share information. A cell phone and a server are both examples of computing devices. These devices are typically connected via physical lines such as fiber optics, although they can also be wireless.

Computer networking is the branch of computer science concerned with the design, architecture, implementation, maintenance, and security of computer networks. It combines computer science, engineering, and telecommunications.

Traffic monitoring systems in cities are an example of a large-scale computer network. These systems provide officials and emergency responders with information on traffic flow and occurrences. A simpler example is using collaboration software like Google Drive to share documents with coworkers who work remotely. A computer network is active whenever we connect via video call, stream movies, share files, communicate using instant messages, or just access something on the internet.

Key Components of Computer Networks

A computer network is made up of two basic components: nodes (network devices) and links. Links connect two or more nodes. Communication protocols determine how these links transport information. The communication endpoints, or origin and destination devices, are commonly referred to as ports.

1. **Network Defense**

    While nodes, connections, and protocols are the building blocks of a network, a contemporary network cannot survive without protection. When massive amounts of data are generated, transferred, and processed over networks, security becomes crucial. Network defense tools include firewalls, intrusion detection systems (IDS), intrusion prevention systems (IPS), network access control (NAC), content filters, proxy servers, anti-DDoS devices, and load balancers.

2. **Communication protocols**

A communication protocol is a collection of rules that all nodes in the information transfer process must follow. Common protocols include TCP/IP, IEEE 802, Ethernet, wireless LAN, and cellular standards. TCP/IP is a conceptual model that defines communication in a modern network. It proposes four functional layers for these communication linkages.

- ❖ **Internet layer:** This layer is in charge of converting data into comprehensible packets and allowing it to be delivered and received.

- ❖ **Network Access Layer:** This layer determines how data is physically conveyed. It describes how hardware transmits data bits over physical cables or fibers.

- ❖ **Transport Layer:** This layer allows devices to continue communication by guaranteeing that the connection is valid and stable.

- ❖ **Application Layer:** This layer specifies how high-level apps can contact the network and initiate data transfers.

The TCP/IP paradigm underpins the majority of modern internet structure, however, the similar but seven-layered open systems interconnection (OSI) model continues to have a significant impact. IEEE802 is a set of IEEE standards that cover local area networks (LAN) and metropolitan area networks (MAN). Wireless LAN is the most well-known member of the IEEE 802 family, sometimes known as WLAN or Wi-Fis.

3. **Links**

    Links are the transmission media and can be of two types:

    ❖ **Wireless:** Network connections can also be made using radio or other electromagnetic signals. This type of transmission is known as 'wireless'. The most prevalent types of wireless links include communication satellites, cellular networks, and radio and technology spread spectrums. Wireless LANs use spectrum technology to make connections over a short region.

    ❖ **Wired:** Wired technologies used in networks include coaxial cables, phone lines, twisted-pair cabling, and optical fibers. Optical fibers carry light pulses that represent data.

4. **Network Devices**

 Network devices, often known as nodes, are computing devices that must be linked to form a network. Several network devices include:

- ❖ **Gateways:** Gateways are hardware devices that serve as 'gates' between two different networks. They could be firewalls, routers, or servers.

- ❖ **Switches:** Repeaters are electrical devices that receive and clean or strengthen network signals, similar to transformers for electricity grids. Hubs are repeaters that have numerous ports. They forward the data to whichever ports are available. Bridges are intelligent hubs that only route data to the desired port. A switch is a multiple-port bridge. numerous data connections can be connected to switches to allow communication with numerous network devices.

- ❖ **Computers, mobile phones, and other consumer electronics:** These are end devices that consumers have direct and regular access to. For example, an email is sent from a laptop or mobile phone's email application.

- ❖ **Routers:** Routing is the process of determining the network path that data packets take. Routers are devices that forward packets between networks until they reach their destination. They help huge networks run more efficiently.

- ❖ **Servers:** These are application or storage servers where the primary computation and data storing take place. All requests for specific actions or data are sent to the servers.

Chapter 3

Key Objectives of Building and Deploying a Computer Network

No industry, including education, retail, banking, technology, government, and healthcare, can function without well-designed computer networks. The network becomes increasingly complex as the size of the organization increases. Before embarking on the onerous effort of designing and establishing a computer network, consider the following main objectives.

Secured remote access.

Computer networks encourage flexibility, which is critical in uncertain times like these when natural disasters and pandemics are sweeping the planet. A secure network ensures that users may safely access and work on sensitive data even when they are not on business premises. Mobile portable devices that are registered with the network can even use multiple layers of authentication to ensure that no bad actors gain access to the system.

Reduction of errors

Networks eliminate errors by guaranteeing that all parties involved obtain information from the same source, even if they are accessing it from separate locations. Back-up data ensures consistency and continuity. A huge number of people can easily access standard versions of customer and employee manuals.

Streamlined collaboration and communication

Networks have a significant impact on the day-to-day operations of a business. Employees may more easily share files, view each other's work, sync calendars, and discuss ideas. Every modern organization uses internal messaging services like Slack to facilitate the free flow of information and conversations. However, emails remain the primary means of professional communication with clients, partners, and vendors.

Increased storage capacity.

Network-attached storage devices are extremely useful for employees who deal with large amounts of data. For example, each member of the data science team does not require individual data stores to handle the massive quantity of records they process. Centralized repositories are even more efficient. With record quantities of client data coming into company systems, the ability to increase storage capacity is critical in today's world.

Cost Savings

Large mainframe computers are an expensive investment; thus, it makes more sense to install processors at critical locations across the system. This not only improves performance but also reduces costs. Networks save operating time and expenses by allowing staff to access information in seconds. Centralized network administration also requires fewer investments in IT support.

Performance Management
The workload of a corporation expands in tandem with its size. When one or more processors are introduced to the network, it improves overall system performance and allows for growth. Saving data in well-designed databases can significantly improve lookup and retrieval speeds.

Resource availability and reliability
A network guarantees that resources are not stored in inaccessible silos and are accessible from various points. The great reliability stems from the fact that there are typically many supply authorities. Important resources must be backed up across many machines to ensure their availability in the event of an incident such as a hardware failure.

Resource sharing

Enterprises today are global in scope, with key assets shared across departments, geographies, and time zones. Clients are no longer limited by location. A network makes data and hardware accessible to all users. This also facilitates interdepartmental data processing. For example, the marketing team examines customer data and product development cycles to help executives make top-level choices.

Types of Computer Networks

Computer networks can be classed depending on a variety of factors, including transmission medium, network size, topology, and organizational goal. On a geographical level, the many types of networks are:

- ❖ **Cloud Network**: A cloud network is a WAN with a cloud-based infrastructure.
- ❖ **Virtual Private Network (VPN):** A VPN is a private network that runs on top of a public network.
- ❖ **Enterprise Private Network (EPN):** An enterprise private network is a single network

that connects a large organization's several office locations.

- **Wide-area networks (WANs):** Wide-area networks connect bigger areas, such as cities, states, and even nations.
- **Metropolitan Area Network (MAN):** MAN is a massive computer network that runs throughout a city.
- **Campus Area Network (CAN):** Campus area networks are made up of interconnected LANs. They are employed by larger organizations like universities and governments.
- **Storage Area Networks (SAN):** A SAN is a specialized network that enables block-level data storage. This is utilized in storage systems like disk arrays and tape libraries.
- **Local Area Network (LAN):** The local area network (LAN) connects devices within a specific geographical area, such as schools, hospitals, and corporate buildings.
- **Personal Area Networks (PAN):** A personal area network (PAN) is a network used by a single

individual to link various devices, such as laptops and scanners.

❖ **Nanoscale networks:** These networks facilitate communication between tiny sensors and actuators.

Networks can be classified based on organizational goals as follows:

❖ **Darknet:** The darknet is an internet-based overlay network that can only be accessed via specialist software. It employs unique, tailored communication protocols.

❖ **Extranet:** An extranet is similar to an intranet, except it includes links to certain external networks. It is typically used to distribute resources across partners, clients, or remote staff.

❖ **Internet:** The internet (or internetwork) is a collection of various networks connected by routers and layered with networking software.

This is a worldwide network that connects governments, researchers, corporations, the general public, and personal computer networks.

- ❖ **Intranet:** An intranet is a collection of networks managed and controlled by a single body. It is generally the most secure sort of network, with access limited to authorized users only. An intranet is often located behind the router in a local area network.

Chapter 4

Best Practices in Computer Network Management

Network management is the process of configuring, monitoring, and troubleshooting everything related to a network, including hardware, software, and connections. Network management comprises five functional areas: fault management, configuration management, performance management, security management, and (user) accounting management. Computer networks can easily become unmanageable behemoths if not properly built and maintained from the start. Here are the best techniques for effective computer network management.

1. **Automate where possible.**

    New devices are frequently introduced to systems, while old ones are discarded. Users and access controls change often. All of this must be automated to prevent human error and the presence of vulnerable zombie systems in the network, which would cost money and compromise security. Automation in terms of security is also important. Automating reactions to assaults, such as banning IP addresses, terminating connections, and obtaining further attack information, is a recommended practice.

2. Consider utilizing honeypots and honeynets.

Honeypots are distinct systems that look to have valid operations and data but are decoys for both internal and outer threats. A breach of this system does not result in the loss of any actual data. A honeynet is a fictitious network segment with the same purpose. While this may incur additional network costs, it enables the security team to monitor for fraudulent players and make necessary adjustments.

3. Use centralized logging.

Centralized logs are critical for getting a comprehensive view of the network. Immediate log analysis can assist the security team in detecting suspicious logins and IT administrators in identifying overburdened systems on the network.

4. **Segregate the network.**

   Enterprise networks can get big and unwieldy. Segregation allows them to be divided into logical or functional components known as "zones." Segregation is typically accomplished with switches, routers, and virtual LAN solutions. One advantage of a segregated network is that it limits the potential damage from a cyberattack while keeping vital resources safe. Another advantage is that it enables better functional classification of networks, such as distinguishing between programmer and human resource demands.

5. **One seller cannot Use numerous vendors to increase security.**

   While it makes sense to stick with a single hardware provider, a wide set of network security technologies is a significant advantage for a large network. Security is a dynamic and ever-changing environment. Hardware developments are quick, and cyber threats change alongside them. One vendor cannot keep up with all threats. Furthermore, different intrusion detection solutions employ various detection algorithms. A good combination of these technologies improves security; nevertheless, you must guarantee that they are interoperable and support common logging and interfacing.

6. Protect the network from insider threats.

Firewalls and intrusion prevention systems keep bad actors out of the network. However, insider risks must also be addressed, especially as cybercriminals use numerous social engineering ploys to target personnel with network access. One approach is to manage and control access using a least-privilege paradigm. Another option is to employ stronger authentication methods, such as single sign-on (SSO) and two-factor authentication (2FA). In addition, personnel must receive frequent training on how to cope with security concerns. Proper escalation procedures must be recorded and widely distributed.

7. Establish baseline network and anomalous behavior.

A baseline enables administrators to understand how the network typically acts in terms of traffic, user access, and so on. With a defined baseline, warnings can be placed in strategic locations to detect anomalies as soon as they occur. The normal range of behavior must be documented at the user and organizational levels. Data for the baseline can be collected from routers, switches, firewalls, wireless APs, sniffers, and dedicated collectors.

8. Use the correct tools.

The network topology is only the first step toward creating a reliable network. To maintain a highly available and dependent network, the necessary tools must be installed in the proper areas. Must-have tools in a network include:

- ❖ **Security Solutions:** Firewalls, content filtering systems, intrusion detection and prevention systems—all of these solutions protect networks carrying more sensitive loads. They are essential components of any network. However, simply having these tools is not enough. They must also be correctly distributed throughout the network. For example, a firewall must be installed at each network junction. Anti-DDoS devices must be put around the network's perimeter. Load balancers should be deployed strategically throughout the system, such as before a cluster of database servers. This must be an explicit component of the network architecture.

- ❖ **IP address managers:** Larger networks require an IP address manager (IPAM) to plan, track, and manage information related to a network's IP addresses.
- ❖ **Configuration Management Tools:** A network has numerous components that communicate with one another. This leads to a large number of setup settings to keep track of. Configuration management technologies address this by providing configuration tools that cover the entire network. They also enable network managers to verify that all compliance standards have been met.

- ❖ **Network Monitoring Solutions:** A network monitoring solution provides full visibility into the network. Visual maps help to assess network performance. It can track packets, provide a detailed view of network activity, and help detect irregularities. Newer monitoring systems use artificial intelligence to predict scaling requirements and cyber dangers based on historical and real-time data.

9. Document and update continuously.

The network's documentation is critical since it serves as the foundation for operations. Documentation must include:

- ✓ A documented record of policies and procedures affecting network operators and users.
- ✓ The software required to enable the hardware and ensure the seamless and secure flow of data
- ✓ Firmware
- ✓ Hardware

✓ Technical standards for equipment, including wires, cables, and connectors

This must be audited at regular intervals or during overhauls. Not only does this simplify network management, but it also enables more efficient compliance assessments.

10. Choose the right topology.

Network topology refers to the pattern or hierarchy by which nodes are linked to one another. The topology can speed up, slow down, or even break the network depending on the company's architecture and requirements. Before creating a network from scratch, network architects must select the appropriate one. Some popular topologies are:

- ❖ **Tree network:** Hierarchical arrangements of nodes are seen below.
- ❖ **Star Network:** A central node server connects to several additional nodes. This is faster since data does not need to pass via each node.
- ❖ **Mesh Network:** Each node must seek to connect with every other node in the system.

- **Ring Network:** Each node connects to two other nodes, making a ring.
- **Bus Network:** Each node is only connected to one other node.

Chapter 5

Network Management Systems' Features and Deployment

A network management system (NMS) functions similarly to a flight control tower, offering a comprehensive picture of the network and assisting with activities such as automation, device identification, monitoring, and troubleshooting. The NMS is also necessary for future planning and development.

One of an NMS's key duties is to identify, configure, monitor, and update networked devices. Furthermore, the use of trustworthy network management software allows for quick real-time performance analysis while also assuring compliance through reporting features. Scalability is another important feature provided by most current NMS systems.

An NMS can be deployed either on-premises or in the cloud. While each has advantages, such as complete resource control for on-premises deployments versus remote server access via the Internet for cloud deployments, the final selection is based on individual organizational requirements and available resources.

Types of network security vulnerabilities. Before delving into various types of security threats and how network security might assist prevent them, it is critical to understand where the network's vulnerability rests. Any weakness allows hackers to gain access to infrastructure, install malware, and steal and manipulate data, as well as delete or erase it. The vulnerabilities include:

- **Unrestricted upload of harmful file types.** Another prevalent sort of network security vulnerability is unrestricted upload of dangerous file types, which occurs when a software allows a hacker to upload and run dangerous files within the software's environment.

- **Missing authentication:** Sometimes the software does not perform any authentication of the user's identity or the resources being used.
- **SQL Injection:** A hacker uses SQL injection to intercept queries sent from an application to its server.
- **Operating-system command injection:** A hacker can execute a random operating system command injection, corrupting the server executing an application, and preventing it from functioning properly.
- **Missing data encryption:** Sometimes software fails to encrypt or safeguard sensitive data before sending or saving it.

Other vulnerabilities include weak passwords, buffer overflows, missing authorization, cross-site scripting and forgery, code downloads without integrity checks, the usage of flawed algorithms, URL redirection to untrusted sites, path traversal, and bugs.

Chapter 6

Common types of networking attacks

Vulnerabilities in the network will expose your firm to a wide range of assaults, including:

1. **Compromise key:** An attacker can gain access to encrypted communication by using a compromised key. This key is typically a secret code or a number that is used to access secure data.

2. **DNS and IP Spoofing:** In domain name system (DNS) spoofing, hackers alter DNS data to insert the attacker's cache. As a result, the name server returns the incorrect IP address during a search. IP spoofing, on the other hand, is a method of impersonating another user by sending packets with incorrect addresses over the internet.

3. **Packet sniffers:** Passive receivers, when placed near a wireless transmitter, make copies of every packet sent. Each packet contains both

confidential and sensitive data. Packet receivers eventually evolve into packet sniffers, extracting all transmitted packets within their range.

4. **Man-in-the-middle:** In this type of assault, a person intercepts and listens to communications between two people across a network. This enables the middleman to capture, monitor, and even control the information to some degree.

5. **Denial of service (DoS) or distributed denial of service (DDoS):** Denial of service (DoS) is the destruction of a single network or even an entire infrastructure, either partially or completely, by denying any authenticated user access. Distributed denial of service (DDoS) is a more advanced kind of DoS that can be difficult to identify and mitigate. Several hacked systems are used to attack the intended victim of the attack. This type of attack also uses botnets.

6. **Botnet:** Malicious software is being sent to a networked collection of private computers. The computers are transformed into zombies, and the attacker has complete control over them. This can happen without the owner's knowledge. The attacker then exploits this control to infect additional devices or cause damage.

7. **Phishing:** Phishing is often related to network attacks. Phishing attacks involve sending emails that appear to be from a recognized and trustworthy source. If a malicious link or attachment is clicked, the network becomes susceptible, and confidential data may be lost.

8. **Worm:** A susceptible network application can be attacked without the user's involvement using a worm. An attacker only needs to use the same internet connection as the user, send malware to the application, and run it. This generates a worm that targets the network.

9. **Malware:** Malware is one of the most efficient methods of propagating malicious attacks. It is specifically designed to destroy the target and get illegal access to a system. Malware primarily copies itself, and because it travels via the Internet, it has access to all networked systems. External devices linked to the network may also be targeted.

10. **Virus:** A virus cannot execute itself and must be activated by the user; the most basic example is an email with a malicious link or attachment. Opening either a link or attachment starts a malicious code, which subsequently bypasses system security mechanisms, rendering them all inoperable. In this situation, the user accidentally corrupts the equipment.

Chapter 7

The Fundamentals of Network Security

When firms consider strategies to improve network security, they typically opt for a multi-layered strategy. Because attacks can occur at any level of a network's configuration, all network hardware, software, and security rules must be designed to address each layer. The principles of network security are:

1. **Administrative network security:**
   Administrative security controls include security rules and practices that govern user behavior. This includes how users are authenticated, the level of access granted to them, and how IT staff members implement infrastructure modifications.

2. **Technical Network Security:** Technical network security safeguards all of the data stored on a network. This can include data that enters, leaves, or transits the network. This is necessary

for two reasons: data must be safeguarded against unauthorized persons as well as malevolent employee activities.

3. **Physical Network Security:** Physical network security prevents unauthorized users from physically accessing components such as routers or cabling cabinets. This is accomplished with the use of locks, biometric authentication, and a variety of additional devices.

4. **Authorization:** Those who request access to specific data on the network are granted authorization after their credentials have been verified.

5. **Accounting:** Accounting keeps track of all actions taken by a user on the network, allowing it to identify both allowed and illegitimate behaviors.

6. **Access Control:** Access control is a system that controls who has access to data.

7. **Identification:** Usernames and identity numbers are used to confirm the identity of users, processes, or devices requesting network access.

8. **Authentication:** Verifying credentials while attempting to log into a network.

Network Security Types and Examples

Let us learn about the many types of network security through examples.

1. **Virtual Private Network (VPN):** VPN creates a secure tunnel for information transmission over the internet. The tunnel is encrypted from the beginning to the end, ensuring that all data sent and received is secure. With telecommuting and working from home becoming more common, employees frequently rely on insecure networks for internet access, making company data exposed to attack. Employees can work from

anywhere in the world while still having access to a secure network that protects company data.

Example: Suppose your company's personnel travel regularly. In that circumstance, they may wind up accessing public WiFi networks. However, if a hacker is utilizing the same network, your employees' systems might be compromised quickly, putting the entire firm at risk. A VPN provides an additional layer of protection by guaranteeing that all communication is encrypted.

2. **Firewalls:** Firewalls are the barriers that separate an internal and external network, such as the Internet. They use a collection of protocols to control incoming and outgoing network traffic. Firewalls form the initial line of defense. If a corporation receives data that does not conform to its specified standards, firewalls prohibit it from passing through.

Example: Firewalls protect traffic at the computer's entrance point, known as ports, where information is shared with external devices. For example, a source address of 165.12.2.1 can reach a destination of 171.14.2.2 over port 22. Only trusted packets with source addresses (165.12.2.1) will be allowed to reach the destination address (171.14.2.2). Aside from that, firewalls prohibit unwanted access to a system and can make your computer invisible when online, preventing attempted breaches in the first place.

3. **DLP (Data Loss Prevention):** Data loss prevention is taking steps to prevent employees from exchanging data outside of a specific network. It ensures that all information is sent securely.

    Example: If an organization collects and stores sensitive personal information and data that are intellectual property or trade secrets, the security level should be high. DLP aids in the secure classification and tagging of data, as well as the detection of odd activity surrounding it, providing an additional layer of protection.

4. **Application Security:** Application security refers to the measures that a developer takes to identify, rectify, and avoid security vulnerabilities at any time throughout the application's development. Applications are not immune to easily exploitable flaws. Application security includes software, hardware, and processes to address any remaining vulnerabilities.

5.

Example: Assume an organization's developers are frequently encountering coding problems. These mistakes could let and accept unverified inputs, potentially leading to SQL injection attacks without anyone realizing. If a hacker discovers them, this can result in even more data leaks. In such cases, implementing application security might benefit the firm.

6. **Email Security:** Email gateways are weak links that frequently lead to security breaches. When phishing attempts are combined with social engineering techniques, emails are the major source of the attacks. With email security, such attacks can be reduced. A secure email gateway, whether on-premises or in the cloud, can prevent such malicious emails from passing through. Email encryption solutions provide security against regulatory violations and data loss.

Example: For example, assume an organization sends emails regularly that contain personally identifiable information such as a name, address, bank account information, or social security number. In this instance, the organization should encrypt its emails with an email security solution.

Exchanging sensitive files or financial information via email is a potentially dangerous activity. This is because most emails are sent in plain text and are not adequately safeguarded as they travel from one server to another. As a result, if businesses use email encryption software, the plain text will be encrypted, making it safer for transmission – because the contents of emails, including attachments, can be intercepted and read by an attacker.

Chapter 8

Challenges of Modern Network Management

Despite its various benefits, network management is not without its own set of challenges. The growing complexity of networks makes efficient management difficult, necessitating the implementation of specific procedures.

- ✓ Adoption of centralized management systems as an efficient solution for dealing with complexity.
- ✓ A deeper understanding and insight into the functioning of the network
- ✓ Implementation of automation processes to improve task-handling efficiency

A dearth of skilled networking specialists exists, which can result in staffing shortages and difficulty in maintaining a stable and reliable network infrastructure. The ongoing growth of technology creates new demands for networks, which may transform how they are maintained through breakthroughs such as artificial intelligence (AI) and machine learn

Conclusion

An effective network improves productivity, security, and creativity while minimizing overhead expenses. This can only be achieved by strong design and implementation, as well as a thorough understanding of the business requirements. While network building may appear to be completely technological, it does require commercial input, particularly in the early stages. Network management also entails adapting workflows and growing and morphing with new technology.

Network security is crucial in a work environment that handles huge amounts of data. A company's capacity to protect crucial information from threats increases client trust and loyalty. It provides business expansion and the flexibility to operate from anywhere in the world safely and securely.

www.ingramcontent.com/pod-product-compliance
Lightning Source LLC
Chambersburg PA
CBHW051535240526
45471CB00020B/2918